I0437646

Thoughts

Across

Time

Thoughts
Across
Time

by Sîrbu Bogdan Alexandru

Copyright © 2009
Sîrbu Bogdan Alexandru

Cover by:
Gergana Todorchovska
Sirbu Bogdan Alexandru

All rights reserved. No part of this book may be reproduced
in any form by any electronic or mechanical means including
photocopying, recording, or information storage and retrieval
without permission in writing from the author.

ISBN: 1441492410
EAN-13: 9781441492418

Book Website
www.tacrosst.com
Email: contact@tacrosst.com

Give feedback on the book at:
feedback@tacrosst.com

Printed in U.S.A

Table of Contents

Watch your thoughts; they become words. Watch your words; they become actions. Watch your actions; they become habits. Watch your habits; they become character. Watch your character; it becomes your destiny.

~ Frank Outlaw

Wisdom vs. Knowledge

My view on knowledge...
Knowledge is important, but non the less Wisdom has a greater meaning, a greater importance.

I always say that:
"Knowledge comes from learning and Wisdom comes from God through learning"

I'm going to ask you a question: Which is more important for you Wisdom or Knowledge?

I can bet that the answer would be "WISDOM" because we all want to be wiser.Being wiser also implies being smarter but in a more special way.

*The question is how
should you be wiser?*

*You don't have to look far to
find the answer, but it's
easier said than done.*

Don't you agree?

*Because it implies changing... and most
of us don't like to change, why? we don't like
to change, because changing in a good way
is harder and does not happen over night.*

It takes time and patience
So my dear friend...
Be wise and finish reading the book...

A loving heart is
the truest wisdom
~Charles Dickens

Wise men talk because
they have something to say.
Fools talk because they
have to say something.

~Plato

To know that you know, and to
know that you don't know -that is
real wisdom.

Without courage, wisdom
bears no fruit.
~Baltasar Gracian

Knowledge is limited.
Wisdom is unlimited.
~ Albert Einstein

You can tell whether a man is clever by his answers. You can tell whether a man is wise by his questions.

~Naguib, Mahfouz

God grant me the serenity to accept the things I cannot change, courage to change the things I can, and wisdom to know the difference.

~The Serenity Prayer (Reinhold Niebuhr)

A wise man can see more from the bottom of a well than a fool can from a mountain top.

~Author Unknown

Science is organized knowledge. Wisdom is organized life.

~Immanuel Kant

A fool sees not the same
tree that a wise man sees.

~ William Blake

Wisdom doesn't necessarily come
with age. Sometimes age
just shows up all by itself.

~Tom Wilson

A single conversation with
a wise man is better than
ten years of study.

~Chinese Proverb

Wisdom is the quality that keeps
you from getting into situations
where you need it.

~Doug Larson

Happy the man who finds wisdom,
the man who gains understanding!
~Proverbs 3:13

These days people seek knowledge,
not wisdom. Knowledge is of the
past, wisdom is of the future.
~Vernon Cooper

Honesty is the first chapter
of the book of wisdom.
~Thomas Jefferson

Wisdom, compassion, and courage
are the three universally recognized
moral qualities of men.

~ Confucius

There is a wisdom of the head,
and... a wisdom of the heart.
~Charles Dickens

If you are wise, it is to your own
advantage; and if you are arrogant,
you alone shall bear it.
~ Proverbs 9:12

The truest greatness lies in being
kind, the truest wisdom
in a happy mind.
~Ella Wheeler Wilcox

A wise person knows that there
is something to be
learned from everyone.
~Unknown

If wisdom and diamonds grew on
the same tree we could soon tell
how much men loved wisdom.
~Lemuel K. Washburn

*

The fool doth think he is wise, but
the wise man knows
himself to be a fool.
~William Shakespeare,

Faith Hope Love

When you realize God is all you have, you realize, God is all you needed in the first place.

Just because you can't see it doesn't mean it isn't there. You can't see the future, yet you know it will come; you can't see the air, yet you continue to breathe.

~ Claire London

Faith is believing in things when common sense tells you not to.

~George Seaton

Faith is raising the sail of our little boat until it is caught up in the soft winds above and picks up speed, not from anything within itself, but from the vast resources of the universe around us.

~W. Ralph Ward

As your faith is strengthened you will find that there is no longer the need to have a sense of control, that things will flow as they will, and that you will flow with them, to your great delight and benefit.

~Emmanuel

Faith enables persons to be persons
because it lets God be God.

~Carter Lindberg

Faith is taking the first step even
when you don't see the
whole staircase.

~Martin Luther King Jr.

Life without faith in something is
too narrow a space to live.

~George Lancaster Spalding

I don't pray for God to take my
problems away, I pray only for
God to give me the strength to go
through them."

- Jose Lozano

Faith is being sure of what we hope
for and certain of what we can't see.
- Hebrews 11:1

And without faith it is impossible
to please him, for he who comes to
God must believe that he is,
and that he is a rewarder of t
hose who seek him.
Hebrews 11:6

A little faith will bring your soul to
heaven, but a lot of faith will
bring heaven to your soul.
~Author Unknown

Faith makes things possible,
not easy.

~Author Unknown

Faith **Hope** Love

Once you choose hope,
anything's possible.
~Christopher Reeve

If one truly has lost hope, one
would not be on hand to say so.
~Eric Bentley

Hope never abandons you,
you abandon it.
~George Weinberg

Things which you do not hope happen more frequently than things which you do hope.
~Titus Maccius Plautus

*

Hope is some extraordinary spiritual grace that God gives us to control our fears, not to oust them.
~Vincent McNabb

When the world says, "Give up,"
Hope whispers,
"Try it one more time."

~Author Unknown

Love floods us with hope.
~Jareb Teague

There is nothing so well known as that we should not expect something for nothing - but we all do and call it Hope.

~Edgar Howe

Hope is that thing with feathers that
perches in the soul and sings
the tune without the words
and never stops... at all.
~Emily Dickinson

Hope begins in the dark, the stub-
born hope that if you just show up
and try to do the right thing,
the dawn will come.

~Anne Lamott

The miserable have no other
medicine.But only hope.

~William Shakespeare,

The road that is built in hope is
more pleasant to the traveler
than the road built in despair,
even though they both lead
to the same destination.
~Marian Zimmer Bradley

Hope is the feeling we have that the feeling we have is not permanent.

~Mignon McLaughlin

Lord save us all from...
a hope tree that has lost the
faculty of putting out blossoms.

~Mark Twain

Hope is faith holding out
its hand in the dark.

~George Iles

When hope is hungry,
everything feeds it.

~Mignon McLaughlin,

The sudden disappointment of a hope leaves a scar which the ultimate fulfillment of that hope never entirely removes.

~Thomas Hardy

Hope is independent of the apparatus of logic.

~Norman Cousins

Sanity may be madness but the maddest of all is to see life as it is and not as it should be.

~Don Quixote

Hope is the only bee that makes honey without flowers.
~Robert Ingersoll

Hope is necessary in every condition. The miseries of poverty, sickness, of captivity, would, without this comfort, be insupportable.

~Samuel Johnson

Hope is the physician
of each misery.

~Irish Proverb

*

Take hope from the heart of man
and you make him a beast of prey.

~Ouida

Hope is like a road in the country;
there was never a road, but when
many people walk on it, the road
comes into existence.
~Lin Yutang

He that lives upon
hope will die fasting.
~Benjamin Franklin,

Hope is putting faith to work when
doubting would be easier.
~Author Unknown

Hope is but the dream of
those who wake.
~Matthew Prior

It is the around-the-corner brand
of hope that prompts people to
action, while the distant hope
acts as an opiate.

~Eric Hoffer

To eat bread without hope is still
slowly to starve to death.
~Pearl S. Buck

Hope is grief's best music.

~Author Unknown

There is no hope unmingled
with fear, and no fear
unmingled with hope.

~Baruch Spinoza

Hope is the word which God has written on the brow of every man.
~Victor Hugo

*

You've gotta have hope. Without hope life is meaningless. Without hope life is meaning less and less.
~Author Unknown

When you say a situation or a person is hopeless, you're slamming the door in the face of God.

~Charles L. Allen

Hope never abandons you, you abandon it.

~George Weinberg

Some see a hopeless end, while others see an endless hope.

~Author Unknown

Hope is the poor man's bread.

~Gary Herbert

Hope is patience with
the lamp lit.
~Tertullian

*

Hope itself is a species of happiness, and, perhaps, the chief happiness which this world affords; but, like all other pleasures immoderately enjoyed, the excesses of hope must be expiated by pain.
~Samuel Johnson

Faith Hope **Love**

Love bears all things, believes all things, hopes all things, endures all things. Love never ends. ~ Bible

The best and most beautiful things in the world cannot be seen or even touched. They must be felt with the heart.

When love is in excess it brings a man no honor nor worthiness.
~Euripides

Like the measles, love is most dangerous when it comes late in life.
~Lord Byron

They do not love that do not show their love. The course of true love never did run smooth. Love is a familiar. Love is a devil. There is no evil angel but Love.
~William Shakespeare

There is only one happiness in life - to love and to be loved.
~George Sand

When you are in Love you can't fall asleep because reality is better than your dreams.
~Dr Seuss

What I needed most was to love and to be loved, eager to be caught. Happily I wrapped those painful bonds around me; and sure enough, I would be lashed with the red-hot pokers or jealousy, by suspicions and fear, by burst of anger and quarrels.
~St. Augustine

For where your treasure is, there your heart will be also.
~Matthew 6:21

Women wish to be loved not because they are pretty, or good, or well bred, or graceful, or intelligent, but because they are themselves.
~Henri Frederic Amiel

You come to love not by finding the perfect person, but by seeing an imperfect person perfectly.
~Sam Keen

Pleasure of love lasts but a moment,
Pain of love lasts a lifetime.
~Bette Davis

To the world you may be one person, but to one person you may be the world.
~Heather Cortez

Love is a canvas furnished by Nature and embroidered by imagination.
~Voltaire

Gravitation is not responsible for people falling in love.
~Albert Einstein

At the touch of love everyone becomes a poet.

~Plato

If you love me, let me know. If not, please gently let me go.
~Anonymous

Life without love is like a tree without blossoms or fruit.
~Kahlil Gibran

The best and most beautiful things in the world cannot be seen or even touched. They must be felt with the heart.
~Helen Keller

The hearth has reasons witch the reason cannot understand.
~ Blaise Pascal

Love does not consist of gazing at each other, but in looking outward together in the same direction.
~Antonic de Saint Excepern

Some love lasts a life time,
thru love lasts forever.
~Unknown Author

There is more hunger for
love and appreciation in this
world than for bread.
~Mother Teresa

And now these three remain:
faith, hope and love. But the
greatest of these is love.
1 Corinthians 13:13

The best and most beautiful things
in the world can not be seen
or even tuched they must be
felt with the hearth.
~Helen Kelle

The hunger for love is much more difficult to remove than the hunger for bread.
~Mother Teresa

Love does not delight in evil but rejoices with the truth.
~Bible

The hearth has reasons witch the reason cannot understand.
~Blaise Pascal

The greatest weakens of most humans is their hesitancy to tell others, how much they love them while they are alive.
~O.A. Battista

Love is patient, love is kind.It does not envy.Love is never boastful, nor conceited, nor rude;It is not self-seeking, nor easily angered.It keeps no record of wrongdoing.It does not delight in evil,But rejoices in the truth.It always protects, trusts, hopes, and preserves.There is nothing love cannot face;There is no limit to its faith, hope, and endurance.In a word, there are three things that last forever:Faith, hope, and love; But the greatest of them all is love.

~1 Corinthians 13:4-7

Practice Forgiveness

The weak can never forgive. Forgiveness is the attribute of the strong. ~Mahatma Gandhi

I can forgive, but I cannot forget, is only another way of saying, I will not forgive. Forgiveness ought to be like a cancelled note – torn in two, and burned up, so that it never can be shown against one.
~Henry Ward Beecher

Forgiveness is the fragrance the violet sheds on the heel that has crushed it.
~Mark Twain

Forgiveness does not change the past, but it does enlarge the future.
~Paul Boese

To forgive is to set a prisoner free and discover that the prisoner was you.
~Lewis B. Smedes,
"Forgiveness – The Power to Change the Past,

You can make up a quarrel, but it will always show where it was patched.
~Edgar Watson Howe,
Country Town Sayings

Forgiveness is the
sweetest revenge.

~Isaac Friedmann

Forgive all who have offended you,
not for them, but for yourself.

~Harriet Nelson

He who cannot forgive breaks
the bridge over which he
himself must pass.

~George Herbert

Nobody forgets where he
buried the hatchet.

~Frank McKinney
"Kin" Hubbard

When you forgive, you in no way change the past – but you sure do change the future.

Forgiveness is a sign that the person who has wronged you means more to you than the wrong they have delt.

~Ben Greenhalgh

It is easier to forgive an enemy than to forgive a friend.
~William Blake, Jerusalem

Forgiveness is a funny thing. It warms the heart and cools the sting.
~William Arthur Ward

One thing you will probably
remember well is any time
you forgive and forget.

~Franklin P. Jones

Never does the human soul appear
so strong as when it forgoes revenge, and dares forgive an injury.

~E.H. Chapin

Always forgive your enemies –
nothing annoys them so much.

~Oscar Wilde

I have learned that sometimes "sor-
ry" is not enough. Sometimes you
actually have to change.

~Claire London

What we forgive too
freely doesn't stay forgiven.

~Mignon McLaughlin,

It's far easier to forgive an enemy
after you've got even with him.

~Olin Miller

There is no revenge so
complete as forgiveness.

~Josh Billings

It's easier to ask forgiveness
than it is to get permission.
~Grace Hopper

Practice simplicity

Life is really simple, but we insist
on making it complicated.

~Confucius

Everything should be made as simple as possible, but not simpler.

~Albert Einstein

A vocabulary of truth and
simplicity will be of
service throughout your life.

The ability to simplify means to
eliminate the unnecessary so that
the necessary may speak.
~Hans Hofmann,

To poke a wood fire is more solid
enjoyment than almost anything
else in the world.
~Charles Dudley Warner

Any intelligent fool can make things
bigger, more complex, and more
violent. It takes a touch of genius -
and a lot of courage - to move in the
opposite direction.
~E.F. Schumacker

Simplicity is making the journey of this life with just baggage enough.

~Author Unknown

*

To find the universal elements enough; to find the air and the water exhilarating; to be refreshed by a morning walk or an evening saunter... to be thrilled by the stars at night; to be elated over a bird's nest or a wildflower in spring - these are some of the rewards of the simple life.

~John Burroughs

The trouble with simple living is
that, though it can be joyful, rich,
and creative, it isn't simple.
~Doris Janzen Longacre

The best things in life are near-
est: Breath in your nostrils, light in
your eyes, flowers at your feet, duties at your hand, the path of right
just before you. Then do not grasp
at the stars, but do life's plain, common work as it comes, certain that
daily duties and daily bread are the
sweetest things in life.

~Robert Louis Stevenson

People love chopping wood.
In this activity one immediately
sees results.

~Albert Einstein

If you cultivate a healthy poverty
and simplicity, so that finding a
penny will literally make your day,
then, since the world is in fact
planted in pennies, you
have with your poverty bought
a lifetime of days.

~Annie Dillard, "Seeing,"
Pilgrim at Tinker Creek, 1974

Be content with what you have, re-
joice in the way things are. When
you realize there is nothing lacking,
the whole world belongs to you.

~Lao Tzu

We don't need to increase our
goods nearly as much as we
need to scale down our wants.
Not wanting something is as good
as possessing it.

~Donald Horban

Frugality is one of the most beautiful and joyful words in the English
language, and yet one that we are
culturally cut off from understanding and enjoying. The consumption
society has made us feel that happiness lies in having things, and has
failed to teach us the happiness of
not having things.
~Elise Boulding

*

There is no greatness where there is
not simplicity, goodness, and truth.
Simplicity is not an objective in art,
but one achieves simplicity despite
one's self by entering into the real
sense of things.

Reduce the complexity
of life by eliminating the
needless wants of life, and the
labors of life reduce themselves.

~Edwin Way Teale

Maybe a person's time would be as
well spent raising food as raising
money to buy food.

~Frank A. Clark

Material blessings, when they pay
beyond the category of need, are
weirdly fruitful of headache.

~Philip Wylie

Live simply that
others might simply live.

~Elizabeth Seaton

Besides the noble art of getting
things done, there is the noble art of
leaving things undone.
The wisdom of life consists in the
elimination of non-essentials.
~Lin Yutang

*

You have succeeded in life
when all you really want is only
what you really need.
~Vernon Howard

As you simplify your life, the laws of the universe will be simpler; solitude will not be solitude, poverty will not be poverty, nor weakness weakness.
~Henry David Thoreau

Have nothing in your houses that you do not know to be useful or believe to be beautiful.
~William Morris

Simplicity is the ultimate sophistication.
~Leonardo DaVinci

Anything simple always interests me.
~David Hockney

Our affluent society contains those of talent and insight who are driven to prefer poverty, to choose it, rather than submit to the desolation of an empty abundance.

~Michael Harrington

How many things are there which I do not want.

~Socrates

I go about looking at horses and cattle. They eat grass, make love, work when they have to, bear their young. I am sick with envy of them.

~Sherwood Anderson

Remember that in giving any reason at all for refusing, you lay some foundation for a future request.

~Arthur Helps

Things to keep in mind

Beginnings are usually scary and endings are usually sad, but it's everything in between that makes it all worth living.~ Sandra Bullock in "Hope Floats"

Dream as if you'll live forever; live as if you'll die tomorrow.
~James Dean

Never look down on anybody unless you're helping him up.
~Jesse Jackson

For every minute you are angry, you lose sixty seconds of happiness.

~Author Unknown

Beauty is not in the face; beauty is a light in the heart.

~Kahlil Gibran

The worth of a book is to be measured by what you can carry away from it.

~James Bryce

You can learn many things from children. How much patience you have, for instance.

~Franklin P. Jones

Great minds have purposes, others have wishes.

~Washington Irving

When we pray to God we must be
seeking nothing - nothing.

~Saint Francis of Assisi

God gives every bird its food, but
He does not throw it into its nest.

~J.G. Holland

What this world needs is a new kind
of army - the army of the kind.

~Cleveland Amory

It is wise to direct your anger
towards problems - not people,
to focus your energies
on answers - not excuses.

~William Arthur Ward

Failure doesn't mean
you are a failure...
it just means you
haven't succeeded yet.

~Robert Schuller

It's better to keep your mouth
shut and give the impression that
you're stupid than to open
it and remove all doubt.

~ Rami Belson

The worth of a book is to be
measured by what you can
carry away from it.

~James Bryce

Beauty is not in the face;
beauty is a light in the heart.

~Kahlil Gibran

Health is not Everything, but Without Health Everything is Nothing

~Dr Bernard Jensen

Each morning when I open my eyes I say to myself: I, not events, have the power to make me happy or unhappy today. I can choose which it shall be. Yesterday is dead, tomorrow hasn't arrived yet. I have just one day, today, and I'm going to be happy in it.

~ Groucho Marx

Some cause happiness wherever they go; others whenever they go.

~Oscar Wilde

Keep your eyes wide open before marriage, half shut afterwards.
~ Benjamin Franklin

It is wise to direct your anger towards problems - not people, to focus your energies on answers - not excuses.
~William Arthur Ward

Failure doesn't mean you are a failure... it just means you haven't succeeded yet.

~Robert Schuller

Shared joy is a double joy; shared sorrow is half a sorrow.

~Swedish Proverb

Truth will set you free

Pretending to be someone your not
is a waste of the person you are.
- Kurt Cobain

The truth hurts for a little
while, but lies hurt forever.
- Eileen Parra

Every man is a moon, and has a
dark side which he never shows
anybody.
~ MarkTwain

I believe that unarmed truth and unconditional love will have the final word in reality. This is why right, temporarily defeated, is stronger than evil triumphant.
~Martin Luther King JR

For where your treasure is, there your heart will be also.
- Matthew 6:21

Everyone wishes to have truth on his side, but not everyone wishes to be on the side of truth.
~Richard Whately

Ye shall know the truth, and the truth shall make you free.
~Bible

If you tell the truth you don't have to remember anything.

Sweet Friendship

A friend is one of the nicest things you can have, and one of the best things you can be.

Friendship is unnecessary, like philosophy, like art.... It has no survival value; rather it is one of those things that give value to survival. ~C.S. Lewis

A single rose can be my garden...
a single friend, my world.
~Leo Buscaglia

If a friend is in trouble, don't annoy him by asking if there is anything you can do. Think up something appropriate and do it.

~Edgar Watson Howe

A true friend never gets in your way unless you happen to be going down.

~Arnold Glasow

The most beautiful discovery true friends make is that they can grow separately without growing apart.

~Elisabeth Foley

A friend knows the song in my heart and sings it to me when my memory fails.

~Donna Roberts

You can always tell a real friend:
when you've made a fool of
yourself he doesn't feel you've
done a permanent job.

~Laurence J. Peter

Friends are those rare people
who ask how you are and then
wait for the answer.

~Author Unknown

It is the friends you can
call up at 4 a.m. that matter.
~Marlene Dietrich

Nothing but heaven itself is better
than a friend who is really a friend.
~Plautus

If instead of a gem, or even a flower,
we should cast the gift of a loving
thought into the heart
of a friend, that would be
giving as the angels give.

~George MacDonald

The friend within the man is that
part of him which belongs to you
and opens to you a door which never, perhaps, is opened to another.
Such a friend is true, and all he says
is true; and he loves you even if he
hates you in other mansions of his
heart.

~Antoine de Saint-Exupéry,
The Wisdom of the Sands

When we honestly ask ourselves which person in our lives mean the most to us, we often find that it is those who, instead of giving advice, solutions, or cures, have chosen rather to share our pain and touch our wounds with a warm and tender hand. The friend who can be silent with us in a moment of despair or confusion, who can stay with us in an hour of grief and bereavement, who can tolerate not knowing, not curing, not healing and face with us the reality of our powerlessness, that is a friend who cares.

~ Henri Nouwen

It takes a long time to
grow an old friend.
~John Leonard

A true friend reaches for your
hand and touches your heart.
~Author Unknown

Friendship is Love,
without his wings.
~Lord Byron, L'Amitié est l'Amour sans Ailes

Strangers are just
friends waiting to happen.
~Rod McKuen, Looking for a Friend

There is one friend in the
life of each of us who seems not a
separate person, however dear and
beloved, but an expansion, an
interpretation, of one's self, the
very meaning of one's soul.
~Edith Wharton

A good friend is a connection
to life - a tie to the past, a road to
the future, the key to sanity
in a totally insane world.

~Lois Wyse

The best time to make
friends is before you need them.
~Ethel Barrymore

There is magic in long-distance
friendships. They let you relate to
other human beings in a way that
goes beyond being physically together and is often more profound.
~Diana Cortes

The most I can do for my
friend is simply be his friend.

~Henry David Thoreau

A friend can tell you things you don't want to tell yourself.

~Frances Ward Weller

Tis a great confidence in a friend to tell him your faults; greater to tell him his.

~Benjamin Franklin

What is a friend? A single soul dwelling in two bodies.

~Aristotle

A true friend is the greatest of all blessings, and that which we take the least care of all to acquire.

~ Francois Duc de La Rochefoucauld

Your friend is the man who knows
all about you, and still likes you.

~ Elbert Hubard

Two are better than one; because they
have a good reward for their labour.
For if they fall, the one will
lift up his fellow: but woe to him that
is alone when he falleth; for he hath
not another to help him up.

~ Bible: Ecclesiastes

The better part of one's
life consists of his friendships.

~Abraham Lincoln

There are big ships and small ships.
But the best ship of all is friendship.

~Author Unknown

But oh! the blessing it is to have
a friend to whom one can speak
fearlessly on any subject; with
whom one's deepest as well
as one's most foolish thoughts
come out simply and safely.
Oh, the comfort - the inexpressible
comfort of feeling safe with a person -
having neither to weigh thoughts nor
measure words, but pouring them all
right out, just as they are, chaff and
grain together; certain that a faithful
hand will take and sift them,
keep what is worth keeping,
and then with the breath of
kindness blow the rest away.

~Dinah Craik

Friendship needs no words -
it is solitude delivered from
the anguish of loneliness.

~Dag Hammarskjold

A friend is someone who
is there for you when
he'd rather be anywhere else.

~ Len Wein

Friendship is the hardest
thing in the world to explain.
It's not something you learn in school.
But if you haven't learned
the meaning of friendship, you
really haven't learned anything.
~ Muhammad Ali

The language of friendship
is not words but meanings.

~Henry David Thoreau

True friends stab
you in the front.
~Oscar Wilde

Love is like the wild-rose briar;
Friendship is like the holly-tree.
The holly is dark when
the rose briar blooms,But which
will bloom most constantly?
~Emily Brontë

What is success?

Success consists of going from failure to failure without loss of enthusiasm. ~Winston Churchill

Some people dream of success...
while others wake up
and work hard at it.
~Author Unknown

God gives every bird its food, but
He does not throw it into its nest.
~J.G. Holland

Try not to become a man
of success, but rather try to
become a man of value.
~Albert Einstein

There are two types of people who
will tell you that you cannot make a
difference in this world: Those who
are afraid to try and those who are
afraid you will succeed.
~ Ray Goforth

To learn to succeed,
you must first learn to fail.
~Michael Jordan

I'm a great believer in
luck, and I find the harder.
I work the more I have of it.
~Thomas Jefferson

Too many people go through life
waiting for things to happen
instead of making them happen!

~Sasha Azevedo

Success is a ladder you
cannot climb with your
hands in your pockets.
~American Proverb

Man stands for long time
with mouth open before
roast duck flies in.
~Chinese Saying

Things may come to those
who wait, but only the things
left by those who hustle.
~Abraham Lincoln

If at first you don't succeed,
Try and try again.

Put your heart, mind, intellect and
soul even to your smallest acts.
This is the secret of success.
~Swami Sivananda

The only place where success comes
before work is in the dictionary.
~Attributed to both Vidal Sassoon
and Donald Kendall

I don't know the key to success, but
the key to failure is to
try to please everyone.

~Bill Cosby

Choose a job you love, and
you will never have to work
a day in your life.
~Confucius

Setting a goal is not the main thing. It is deciding how you will go about achieving it and staying with that plan. ~Tom Landry

The only thing that can stop
you is the doubt that
you carry in your mind.
~Chae Richardson

The real secret of success
is enthusiasm.
~Walter Chrysler

The toughest thing about
success is that you've got to keep
on being a success
~Irving Berlin

Success is counted sweetest
By those who ne'er succeed.
To comprehend a nectar
Requires sorest need.
~Emily Dickinson

I do not pray for success.
I ask for faithfulness.
~Mother Teresa

Coming together is a beginning.
Keeping together is progress.
Working together is success.
~Henry Ford

I can't change the direction of the
wind, but I can adjust my sails to
always reach my destination.
~Jimmy Dean

The secret of success is this:
there is no secret of success.

~Elbert Hubbard

The successful person has the habit of doing the things failures don't like to do. They don't like doing them either necessarily. But their disliking is subordinated to the strength of their purpose. ~E. M. Gray

Put your heart, mind, intellect and soul even to your smallest acts. This is the secret of success.

~Swami Sivananda

Ability may get you to the top, but it takes character to keep you there.

God gives every bird a worm, but he does not throw it into the nest.

There are no shortcuts
to any place worth going.
~ Helen Keller

Opportunity is missed by most
people because it is dressed
in overalls and looks like work.
~Thomas Edison

God gave us two ends - one to sit on
and one to think with. Success de-
pends on which one you use.
Head you win, tail you lose.

~Author Unknown

My Thoughts

Dear reader feel encouraged to lay all your thoughts
on these blank pages of this chapter.

www.ingramcontent.com/pod-product-compliance
Lightning Source LLC
Chambersburg PA
CBHW031235280526
45784CB00004B/1578